COMBAT

by Jason Page

A BIG HIT

A boxer scores points for hitting his opponent on the front or side of his torso or the front or side of his head.

adidas

COMBAT EVENTS

Competitors in the Olympic events described in this book really have to fight for a medal!

ANCIENT ORIGINS

Combat sports were among the most popular events at the ancient Olympic Games. They included boxing and wrestling matches, as well as a brutal fighting sport called the *pankration*. This was a form of hand-to-hand combat in which almost anything was permitted.

Taekwondo

SUPER STATS

Some 15,000 people packed into the Nippon Budokan Hall in Tokyo to watch the finals of the first Olympic judo competition in 1964. It would have taken 307 buses to drive everyone home!

WARNING!

Combat sports are dangerous! Even well-trained athletes can be seriously injured competing in the events shown in this book. Never try to perform a combat technique without expert supervision.

MODERN GAMES

Carl Schuhmann

Combat events been part of the modern Games ever since they began. This picture shows the two heavyweight finalists in the Greco-Roman wrestling competition at the first modern Olympics. Carl Schuhmann (GER) defeated Georgis Tsitas (GRE) and won the gold medal.

OLYMPICS FACT FILE

The Olympic Games were first held in Olympia, Greece, around 3,000 years ago. They took place every four years until they were abolished in A. D. 393.

A Frenchman named Pierre de Coubertin (1863–1937) revived the Games, and the first modern Olympics were held in Athens in 1896.

The modern Games have been held every four years since 1896, except in 1916, 1940, and 1944 because of war. Special 10th-anniversary Games took place in 1906.

The symbol of the Olympic Games is five interlocking colored rings. They represent the five different continents from which athletes come to compete.

NEW FOR 2000

At the Sydney Games, medals will be awarded for the first time in taekwondo, one of two new Olympic sports making their debuts.

Giovanna Trillini

TEAM EFFORT

Giovanna Trillini (ITA) celebrates victory in the women's team foil at the 1996 Games. As well as individual competitions, there are team events for both men and women in the foil and épée and for men in the sabre. Each team is made up of three fencers from the same country.

DID YOU KNOW?

After arguing over the result of the men's team foil event, fencers at the 1924 Olympics fought two real duels!

The first sword-fighting competitions were held more than 5,000 years ago in ancient Japan and Egypt.

Despite being deaf, Ildikó Sagi-Retjö (HUN) proved what an exceptional competitor she was when she won a total of seven fencing medals at five Olympic Games between 1960 and 1976.

The foil has a rectangular blade almost 3 feet (90 cm) long.

CHOOSE YOUR WEAPON

You can tell the different swords apart by looking at their hand guards or the shape of their blades.

DUEL PURPOSE

Fencing began as a way of practicing the sword-fighting skills needed for duels. Until the 1800s, arguments between noblemen were often settled by swords or pistols. These duels were sometimes fought to the death!

FENCING: FOIL

There are three different fencing disciplines, and each one uses a different sword. First up is the foil.

RULE BOOK: FOIL

Fencers score points by touching their opponents with their swords. In foil events, they must aim for their opponent's trunk — hits to the head, arms, or legs don't count — and must strike with the tip of the foil not the side. They can only score a hit with an attacking move. If they hit their opponent while defending themselves no points are scored.

The épée is the same length as the foil but has a larger hand guard and a triangular blade.

The sabre has a V-shaped blade 34 inches (88 cm) long and a curved hand guard to protect the fencer's knuckles.

SUPER STATS

France has won more fencing medals than any other nation. French fencers have notched 104 medals. Italy is in second place with 97, while Hungary comes in third with 78.

FENCING: ÉPÉE

The épée is the modern fencing equivalent of the rapier—a razor-sharp sword that was used in deadly duels!

RULE BOOK: ÉPÉE

In épée (EH pay) events, fencers score a point for hitting any part of their opponent's body. It doesn't matter whether they are attacking or defending themselves at the time. However, as in the foil events, they must strike with the tip, not the side, of the sword.

Fencers do not wear clothes with buckles or straps because these could snag on a sword.

Épée fencing

LEARN THE LINGO

Fencers wear a padded glove on the hand that holds their sword.

Get your tongue around some of fencing's technical terms:

Lunge: an attack in which the sword is thrust forward

Parry: defensive stroke to deflect the attacker's sword

Riposte: an attack that follows a defensive move

Touché!: shouted out when one competitor scores a hit

STARTER'S ORDERS

At the beginning of each bout, the director (umpire) shouts "En garde!" The two fencers raise their swords. Then he or she calls out "Allez!" which is the signal to start fighting.

Épée fencing, Olympic Games, 1928

A mask with a metal grill prevents injuries to the fencer's head and face.

HITTING THE SPOT

This picture was taken at the Games in 1928. The person standing in the middle is the umpire or "director," who judges each bout. An electronic scoring system was used for the first time at the Olympics in 1956. It automatically detected when one of the competitors scored a hit, making the umpire's job much easier. All Olympic fencing matches are scored electronically.

Underneath the jacket is a sturdy vest called a plastron that protects the fencer's chest.

Traditionally, fencers wear white clothes.

DRESS CODE

Although fencing swords have blunted tips, they can still cause serious injuries. This is why all competitors wear tough protective clothing.

DID YOU KNOW?

⟫ Even with all the right safety equipment, fencing is still dangerous. In 1982, one of the reigning Olympic champions died after a sword went through his mask.

⟫ Fencers stand sideways from each other to present a smaller area for their opponent to strike.

⟫ The épée is the heaviest fencing sword. It weighs up to 1.5 times the weight of the foil or sabre.

GOLDEN GREAT

Aladár Gerevich (HUN) was the greatest Olympic fencer ever. He won seven gold medals in the sabre events, plus a silver and two bronzes (one in foil), between 1932 and 1960. Gerevich is the only person from any sport to win golds in six successive Games.

Aladár Gerevich

DID YOU KNOW?

Fencers salute each other before a bout by raising the hand guards of their swords to their chins and swiftly snapping them down.

Fencing has been part of every single modern Olympic Games.

The gold medal in the men's individual sabre was won by a fencer from Hungary at every Olympic Games from 1924 to 1964.

En garde line: Fencers must stand on either side of this line at the beginning of each bout.

Rear limit line: Fencers are not allowed to step over this line.

The lights are part of the electronic scoring system.

LIGHT WORK

The electronic scoring system uses colored lights to indicate when one fencer has scored a hit against his opponent. A red or green light means that a valid point has been scored. A white light means the blow landed outside the target area.

FENCING: SABRE

Unlike the other two fencing disciplines, the sabre events are for men only.

Sabre fencing

Warning lines show fencers when they are close to the rear limit.

RULE BOOK: SABRE

When fencing with a sabre, as in foil events, fencers only score points for attacking moves. However, unlike both the foil and the épée, fencers are allowed to strike with the side as well as the tip of a sabre.

GET IN LINE

Fencers compete on a narrow mat, called a piste, 46 feet (14 meters) long and 4.9 feet (1.5 meters) wide, marked with a series of lines.

ANIMAL OLYMPIANS

The fencing gold at the Animal Olympics goes to the swordfish. Like human fencing champions, the swordfish is very fast, with a top speed of 37 mph (60 km/h). The sword on the front of its head is actually an elongated tooth, and it can measure more than 3 feet (1 meter) in length!

Men's team sabre: Russia

MARTIAL ARTS

Traditional fighting skills from Far Eastern countries are known as martial arts. They include the two Olympic sports of judo and taekwondo.

MAKING THE GRADE

People who learn judo or taekwondo wear different colored belts to show what grade they have reached.

Lowest grade

TAEKWONDO

Highest grade

Lowest grade

JUDO

Highest grade

Taekwondo

ANCIENT INSPIRATION

Judo was invented in 1892 by a Japanese teacher named Dr. Jigoro Kano, four years before the first modern Olympic Games were held. Dr. Kano based judo on an ancient martial art, called jujitsu, practiced by Samurai warriors 1,000 years ago.

BLOW BY BLOW

Taekwondo is a martial art from Korea. In Korean, tae means "punch," kwon means "kick," and do means "art," so taekwondo means the art of kicking and punching—which is exactly what it is! Competitors score points by striking their opponent using their hands and feet.

DID YOU KNOW?

Judo became an Olympic sport for the first time in 1964, when the Games were held in Tokyo.

There are lots of other martial arts, including karate and aikido (from Japan), kung fu (from China), escrima (from the Philippines), and pentjak silat (from Malaysia).

Wall paintings found in the 2,000-year-old tomb of a Korean king show people practicing a form of fighting that looks just like taekwondo.

GENTLY DOES IT

The word "judo" in Japanese means "the gentle way." Some jujitsu techniques can cause serious injuries, but Dr. Kano left all of these aggressive moves out of judo. Punching and kicking are against the rules. Instead, contestants earn points by throwing or holding their opponent on the ground.

GOING FOR GOLD

Taekwondo was a demonstration sport at the Olympics in 1988 and 1992. It will be a full Olympic sport when the Games come to Sydney. This means that medals will be awarded for the first time in taekwondo events. You can find out more about this sport on pages 16–19.

JUDO

Not surprisingly, Japan has dominated the men's judo events, winning more than twice as many gold medals as any other country.

WEIGHT FOR IT

Fighting sports such as martial arts, wrestling, and boxing are divided into weight categories so that all the contestants compete against people their own size.

There are seven different men's judo events at the Olympics.

GROUND WORK

Here, Tadahiro Nomura (JPN) is grappling with Girolamo Giovinazzo (ITA) at the 1996 Olympics, each contestant trying to get his opponent's shoulders down against the mat.

A contestant earns more points the longer he can hold his opponent down. If he holds his opponent down for 30 seconds, he wins the match.

Tadahiro Nomura

David Douillet

> *David Douillet (FRA) is the reigning men's heavyweight champion. He will be competing in Sydney.*

> *The suit worn by judokas is called a "gi." It consists of a simple jacket and trousers, and is made of sturdy material so that it doesn't rip.*

FRANCE

Competitors are not allowed to wear shoes.

DID YOU KNOW?

- *Yasuhiro Yamashita (JPN), who won a gold medal at the Olympics in 1984, went on to compete in 203 fights without being defeated.*

- *People who learn judo are called judokas.*

- *Theodore Roosevelt, who became president of the United States in 1901, was one of the first people in the U. S. to learn judo. He eventually earned his brown belt!*

Fighters in competitions wear two belts. One shows which grade they have reached. The other is either a white or red belt so that the referee can tell who's who.

WHAT'S THE POINT?

Judo contests consist of single fights rather than a series of rounds. In each judo contest, a referee and two judges award points and partial points for throws and holds. For example, a perfect throw, in which a contestant is hurled flat on his back, is worth a point (or "ippon") and automatically wins the match.

SUPER STATS

The largest competitor ever in an Olympic judo competition was Jong Gil Pak (PRK), who took part in the 1976 Games. Pak was 7 feet (2.13 meters) tall and weighed 359 pounds (163 kg). That's more than five times as heavy as you!

JUDO (CONTINUED)

Marie-Claire Restoux

Women competed in judo events for the first time in 1992. There are seven weight classes for women, the same number as for men.

Tamura Ryoko

GIVE UP YET?

Armlocks and strangleholds can be used to force an opponent to submit. If a competitor cannot get out of a hold, she can surrender by tapping the mat several times with her hand. After this picture was taken at the 1996 Games, Marie-Claire Restoux (FRA) managed to escape from her opponent's clutches and went on to win a gold medal.

LEARN THE LINGO

Judo's technical terms are all in Japanese.

Dojo: a training hall
Hajime: begin fighting
Rei: bow
Senshu: a judo champion
Sore-made: the contest is over

THE BIG BANG

When contestants are thrown during a judo contest, they usually hit the mat with a loud bang. However, it's not nearly as painful as it sounds! In fact, the noise is made by competitors slapping their arm against the mat. This technique breaks their fall and actually prevents serious injuries.

NICE THROW

Tamura Ryoko (JPN) throws Kye Sun (PRK) during the women's extra-lightweight final at the 1996 Olympic Games, at left. Tamura took second place at Atlanta but is a strong contender for a gold medal in Sydney. In 1999, she became the women's extra-lightweight world champion for the fourth time in a row!

DID YOU KNOW?

Before each judo match begins, the contestants bow to the referee and each other as a sign of respect.

Tamura's defeat at the 1996 Games was her first defeat in 84 matches.

Judo is the only Olympic sport in which competitors are allowed to break each other's arms!

BATTLE ZONE

Competitors must stay inside the contest area when they are fighting. This measures 7 yards (6 meters) square and is surrounded by a red border to warn the competitors when they are getting too close to the edge. The floor inside the contest area is covered by a firm rubber mat.

lightweight (125 lb/57 kg): Driulis Gonzalez (CUB) half-middleweight (139 lb/63 kg): Yuko Emoto (JAP) middleweight (155 lb/70 kg): Cho Min-sun (KOR) half-heavyweight (175 lb/78 kg): Ulla Werbrouck (BEL) heavyweight (over 175 lb/78 kg): Sun Fuming (CHN)

SMASHING TIME

A traditional part of taekwondo training is called "kyukpa," which means "breaking." This involves smashing planks of wood, tiles, and even bricks using only the fists, elbows, feet, and hands. Kyukpa is not done just to impress. It is an important practice technique and a way of testing precision and power. It takes years to master — don't be tempted to try it at home!

Kyukpa

DID YOU KNOW?

There are four different weight categories in the Olympic taekwondo competition.

A contestant is automatically disqualified if he or she receives three penalty points.

Each taekwondo contest is made up of three rounds (called "jeons") and each round lasts for three minutes.

JOO WHO?

"Joo-sim" is the name given to the referee. The referee is assisted by four judges — one on each corner of the fighting area. The judges award the contestants a point every time they land a legal blow on their opponent and deduct a point for each foul they commit.

Starting a taekwondo contest

Taekwondo is a new Olympic sport that will be contested for the first time at the Sydney Olympics in 2000.

TAEKWONDO

Competitors from North and South Korea seem certain to do well in the men's taekwondo competition—it is their national sport, after all!

RULE BOOK

In taekwondo, contestants are only allowed to attack the front part of their opponent's body and can only use punches and kicks. The throws used in judo, for example, are strictly forbidden. All punches must be above the waist, and kicks are only allowed when attacking the opponent's head.

STARTER'S ORDERS

At the start of a taekwondo contest, the referee shouts "cha-ryeot," the command for both contestants to stand at attention. When the referee shouts "kyeong-rye," both contestants bow. Finally, the referee shouts out "shi-jak," which is the signal to start fighting.

SUPER STATS

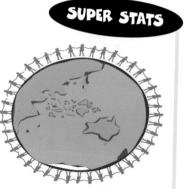

Taekwondo is practiced by about 50 million people in 160 different countries all over the world. If everyone who did taekwondo joined hands, they could form a line that would stretch around the middle of the Earth 1.25 times!

TAEKWONDO
(CONTINUED)

With four women's weight categories in the taekwondo events, it's not just the men who pack a punch at the Olympics!

> Pads must be worn under the dubok to protect the competitor's shins, groin, and forearms.

COLOR CODE

To help the referee identify the competitors, contestants have different colored markings on their body pads. One wears red ("hong"), the other blue ("chung"). These markings also show the three target areas on the competitor's body that their opponent must aim for. Blows outside these areas (apart from blows to the head) incur penalties.

> A padded body guard is worn over the chest to soften kicks and punches.

Taekwondo competitors

LEARN THE LINGO

A quick guide to some more of taekwondo's tricky terminology:

Dung-joomock chi-gi: back-fist punch

Dwi cha-gi: back kick

Palkoop chi-gi: elbow punch

Sob-nal chi-gi: knife-hand punch

Yop cha-gi: side kick

Taekwondo is a new Olympic sport that will be contested for the first time at the Sydney Olympics in 2000.

A plastic safety helmet protects the competitor's head.

QUICK THINKING

Fighting sports such as taekwondo aren't just about attacking your opponent. They are also about defending yourself, and competitors need lightning-quick reactions! In this picture, Mi Sun Kim (KOR), fighting in blue, leans back quickly and just manages to dodge a kick from her opponent, Kelly Thorpe (USA).

Mi Sun Kim (KOR)

Colored marks identify each competitor and mark target areas for hitting.

PENALTY POINTS

Grabbing, pushing, or tripping an opponent is against the rules and results in a penalty point. The same applies when a contestant deliberately steps outside the contest area or turns his or her back toward his or her opponent.

The white suit worn by the competitors is known as a dubok. It is made of a lighter material than the suit worn in judo.

DID YOU KNOW?

There will be 100 competitors (52 men, 48 women) trying to win the first eight taekwondo Olympic gold medals, which will be awarded in Sydney.

As in boxing, if a contestant is knocked down and does not get up within 8 seconds, his or her opponent automatically wins the contest.

The competition area is a 26-foot (8-meter) blue square mat.

This means that no Olympic record has yet been set.

DID YOU KNOW?

🥊 Boxing events were not held at the 1912 Olympics because the sport was against the law in Sweden, which is where the Games were held that year!

🥊 At the beginning of a match, the two competitors shake hands by touching their gloves together.

🥊 At the 1996 Olympic Games, Cuban boxers won gold or silver medals in 7 out of the 12 events!

Somick Kamsing

HANDS UP!

At the end of a match, both boxers stand in the center of the ring, one on either side of the referee. The referee then raises the winner's arm up into the air to show the spectators who has won. This picture was taken after Somick Kamsing (THA) defeated Serafim Todorov (BUL) in the featherweight final at the 1996 Games.

WEIGH TO GO

There are 12 Olympic boxing events. Boxers fight in the event appropriate to their weight. This chart shows the maximum weight for each event.

BOXING WEIGHT CATEGORIES

Light-flyweight: 106 lb (48 kg) Flyweight: 112 lb (51 kg)
Bantamweight: 119 lb (54 kg) Featherweight: 126 lb (57 kg)
Lightweight: 132 lb (60 kg) Light-welterweight: 140 lb (63.5 kg)
Welterweight: 148 lb (67 kg) Light-middleweight: 157 lb (71 kg)
Middleweight: 165 lb (75 kg) Light-heavyweight: 179 lb (81 kg)
Heavyweight: 201 lb (91 kg) Super-heavyweight: over 201 (91 kg)

BOXING

The first recorded boxing event at the Olympic Games took place in 688 B. C. The contestants wrapped strips of leather around their hands and fought each other until one competitor was knocked unconscious!

CLOSE SHAVE

There are strict rules about who can take part in boxing events at the modern Olympics. For a start, all competitors must be men — there are no Olympic boxing events for women. Boxers must also be over 17 years old but under 34, for health reasons. Another rule says that competitors can't compete if they have beards!

GIVE US A RING

Boxing matches take place in what's called a "ring," although it's actually square in shape! The ring is surrounded by four elastic ropes, and each side is 20 feet (6 meters) long. Two corners of the ring are colored: one is red, one is blue (one for each opponent). The other two are white (neutral).

ANIMAL OLYMPIANS

It's not just humans who like to box — kangaroos do too! Young kangaroos often play at boxing each other with their front paws. However, you wouldn't want to get into a real fight with a kangaroo. A blow from one of their back legs is powerful enough to kill.

bantamweight: Istvan Kovacs (HUN) **featherweight:** Somick Kamsing (THA)

BOXING (CONTINUED)

Modern boxing rules are based on the "Queensbury rules," drawn up in the 1800s, which stated that all boxers should wear proper leather gloves!

Boxing rules

BUTTON IT!

Olympic boxing matches are scored by a panel of five judges using an electronic scoring system. Each judge has two buttons in front of him, one for each boxer. Every time he thinks that one of the boxers has scored a point, he presses the appropriate button. However, the boxer doesn't get the point unless at least two other judges agree and have also pressed their buttons.

All Olympic boxers must wear protective headgear.

Professional boxers fight bare chested, but Olympic boxers must wear tank tops when competing.

SUPER STATS

The United States is the most successful boxing nation. In 19 Games, the U. S. has produced 46 Olympic champions. Cuba is second with 21 gold medals, while the former Soviet Union and Italy are tied for third with 14.

Long lace-up boots support the boxer's ankles and help him grip the mat.

Boxers wrap their hands in bandages and wear padded gloves for protection.

László Papp

GOING FOR THE TRIPLE

In 1956, László Papp (HUN) became the first boxer ever to win three Olympic gold medals. This feat was equaled by Teofilo Stevenson (CUB) in 1980. It could happen again in Sydney for another Cuban, Felix Savon (see pages 24–25), who is going for his third Olympic victory in a row.

Boxers' shorts must have a clear "beltline." If their opponent hits them below this, it is counted as a foul.

A DIRECT HIT

The judges only award a point to a boxer if he hits his opponent on the front or side of his torso or the front or side of his head. Blows to his opponent's arms don't count. To be valid, a punch must be made with the knuckles of the glove and, in the judges' opinion, be powerful. Blows with no force behind them don't count.

DID YOU KNOW?

Boxing is probably the most dangerous of all Olympic sports, and some people believe it should be banned.

Three doctors are required to attend every Olympic fight.

In 1908, Reg Baker (AUS) made it to the final of the Olympic middleweight contest, not bad considering he was also a member of the Australian swimming and diving teams!

DID YOU KNOW?

The ancient Greeks had their own Olympic boxing heroes too—men such as Theagenes from Thasos, who won the boxing event almost 2,500 years ago in 480 B.C.

The referee shouts "seconds away" before the start of each round to tell the seconds (see right) to get out of the ring.

If a coach wants to stop the fight and withdraw his boxer, he simply throws a towel into the ring.

BREATHING SPACE

Between rounds the boxers return to their corners and are allowed one minute of rest. During this time, their coaches and "seconds" (the coaches' assistants) are allowed to give them advice and tend to injuries. Here, four-time world heavyweight champion, Felix Savon (CUB), takes a rest.

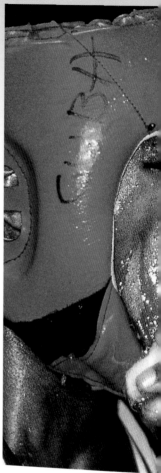

Cassius Clay

BIG HITS

Boxing champions such as George Foreman (USA), Joe Frazier (USA), and Lennox Lewis (CAN) were all Olympic gold medalists. The famous Cassius Clay (now known as Muhammad Ali, USA) is seen here with his gold medal in 1960.

BOXING
(CONTINUED)

Many boxers won gold medals at the Olympics before achieving even greater success and fame as professional boxers.

ALL CHANGE

Previously, Olympic boxing matches consisted of three rounds lasting 3 minutes each. At Sydney, this has been changed to four 2-minute rounds. The beginning and end of each round is signaled by ringing a bell.

LEARN THE LINGO

These boxing terms are a knockout!

Jab: a short, quick punch

Lead arm: the arm the boxer uses to jab his opponent

Southpaw: a left-handed boxer who jabs with his right arm

Sparring: practice fights

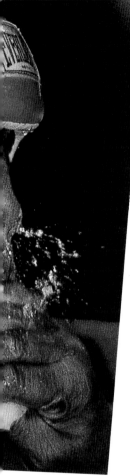

Felix Savon

AND THE WINNER IS...

Boxers can win an Olympic boxing match by scoring more points than their opponent or by a knockout, which is when a boxer knocks down his opponent so he is unable to get up within 10 seconds (as counted by the referee). A competitor can also withdraw from the match or be withdrawn by the referee or his own coach if they feel he is in danger of being injured. And boxers can be disqualified for committing a foul!

heavyweight: Felix Savon (CUB) **super-heavyweight**: Vladimir Klichko (UKR)

WRESTLING

There are two different wrestling disciplines—Greco-Roman and freestyle—with eight events in each.

The same mat is used in both forms of wrestling. The mat is at least 1.6 inches (4 cm) thick and is raised to give spectators a better view.

RULE BOOK

In both Greco-Roman and freestyle wrestling, competitors are awarded points for throws and holds performed on their opponent. The contestant with the most points at the end of the match wins. A wrestler can also win by opening up a 10-point lead or managing to pin his opponent's shoulder blades against the mat for half a second.

The central circle is a small yellow ring in the middle of the mat where the wrestlers start each bout.

The safety zone is blue and must be at least 4.9 feet (1.5 meters) wide. Wrestlers may not cross into this zone.

Soviet Union	68
USA	46

SUPER STATS

Competitors from the former Soviet Union have won 68 victories in wrestling events. The United States is second with 46 victories, although it has won only two gold medals in the Greco-Roman wrestling events.

The weight categories for wrestling will change at the Sydney Olympics. There will be just 8 categories instead of the 10 included in previous Games.

The passivity zone is a red border 39 inches (1 meter) thick that shows the wrestlers they are approaching the edge of the mat.

NO LEGS!

In Greco-Roman wrestling, unlike freestyle wrestling, competitors are not allowed to attack their opponent's legs or use their own legs to attack him.

wrestling mat

DID YOU KNOW?

Only two people have won a gold medal in both wrestling styles at the same Games.

The most medals ever won by a wrestler is five. Wilfred Dietrich (GER) won one gold, two silvers, and two bronzes between 1956 and 1968.

Wrestling is a men-only event at the moment but there are plans to introduce women's wrestling events in 2004.

Most of the action takes place in the central area, which is yellow and is 23 feet (7 meters) wide.

TIME FOR CHANGE

Modern wrestling bouts consist of two three-minute rounds with three minutes of extra time in the event of a draw. However, until 1924, competitions had no time limits. In 1912, Martin Klein (RUS) and Alfred Asikáinen (FIN) wrestled for 11 hours and 40 minutes. Klein eventually won but was too exhausted to compete in the final!

Martin Klein & Alfred Asikáinen

The new categories will include: 54 kg, 58 kg, 63 kg, 69 kg, 76 kg, 85 kg, 97 kg, and 130 kg.

DID YOU KNOW?

? Only one Greek competitor has won a gold medal in the Greco-Roman wrestling!

? The greatest wrestler in ancient times was a man known as Milon of Croton, who won five Olympic golds between 532 and 516 B. C.

? In ancient times, wrestlers were allowed to rub oil on their bodies to make their skin slippery. This is forbidden in modern wrestling contests.

BUILDING A BRIDGE

One of the classic defensive moves in Greco-Roman wrestling is known as the "bridge," and it requires great strength. In this move, the wrestler arches his back and balances on his head and toes to stop his opponent from pinning his shoulders to the mat. Pasquale Passarelli (FRG), in the bantamweight final in 1984, managed to hold this position for 96 seconds and won the gold medal.

Yuriy Melnichenko (KAZ) & Denis Hall (USA)

Alexander Karelin

WANT A LIFT?

The reigning heavyweight champion, Alexander Karelin (RUS), is seen here fighting Siamak Ghaffar (USA) at the 1996 Olympics. Karelin is one of the strongest men ever to compete at the Games. He specializes in a move known as the Karelin Lift, in which he picks up his opponent and throws him over his head!

REIGNING OLYMPIC CHAMPIONS: **48 kg:** Sim Kwon-Ho (KOR) **52 kg:** Armen Nazaryan (ARM) **57 k:** Yuriy Melnichenko (KAZ) **62 k:** Wlodzimierz Zawadzki (POL) **68 kg:** Ryszard Wolny (POL

GRECO-ROMAN WRESTLING

Lifts, throws, tumbles, and turns—it's hard to keep your feet on the ground when you're a Greco-Roman wrestler!

RULE BOOK

Wrestlers are awarded one point for a takedown (forcing an opponent down on to the mat), two points for turning an opponent over so his back is on the mat, three points for taking an opponent off his feet and turning him over all in one move, and five points for throwing an opponent in the air.

Check out these traditional wrestling terms:

LEARN THE LINGO

Fall: pinning the opponent's shoulders to the ground

Takedown: overpowering the opponent and gradually forcing him to the ground.

Tomber: this is the French word for "fall." If a wrestler can hold his opponent's shoulders down for as long as it takes the referee to say "tomber" (1 second), he wins the match.

NOT TO BE SNIFFED AT!

One of the more unusual wrestling rules says that all competitors in Greco-Roman events must have a handkerchief tucked into their clothing! This dates back to when wrestlers had to wipe blood or sweat off their bodies. Modern wrestlers use antiseptic sprays.

74 kg: Feliberto Aguilera (CUB) **82 kg:** Hamza Yerlikaya (TUR) **90 kg:** Vyacheslav Oleynyk (UKR) **100 kg:** Andrzej Wronski (POL) **130 kg:** Alexander Karelin (RUS)

FREESTYLE WRESTLING

For wrestling that's fast and furious,
check out the freestyle events!

FAIR GAMES

Freestyle wrestling became popular in Great Britain and
the United States during the 1800s because it's faster
and more dramatic than the traditional Greco-Roman
style. Known as "catch as catch can," freestyle
contests were often held at fairs and festivals.
Freestyle events were held at the Olympic
Games for the first time in 1904.

SUPER STATS

The heaviest competitor in
Olympic history was a
freestyle wrestler named
Chris Taylor (USA), who
won a bronze medal at
the Games in 1972.
Taylor weighed 419
pounds (190 kg). That's
about three times as
heavy as most adults!

Wrestlers
wear a leotard
that leaves their
shoulders bare.

LEG IT!

Grabbing an opponent's legs, as the wrestler wearing red is doing in this picture, is permitted in freestyle contests. Tripping an opponent or holding him with one's legs is also allowed.

Townsend Saunders (USA) & Vadin Bogiev (RUS)

One wrestler wears red, the other blue, to help the referee identify them.

RULE BOOK

In a wrestling match, competitors are not allowed to pull their opponent's hair or ears, twist his fingers, or touch his face. Biting, pinching, kicking, punching, and striking with the elbow are also forbidden, as is holding on to an opponent by his clothes.

DID YOU KNOW?

In 1980, the Beloglazov twins (URS) both won gold medals in the freestyle. At the 1984 Games, the Schultz twins (USA) repeated the feat!

In 1904, all seven freestyle events were won by wrestlers from the United States—the only nation with competitors!

Wrestlers are not allowed to talk to each other during a bout.

INDEX

Acknowledgments
We would like to thank Ian Hodge, Rosalind Beckman, Jackie Gaff and Elizabeth Wiggans for their assistance. Cartoons by John Alston.
Copyright © 2000 *ticktock* Publishing Ltd. Printed in Hong Kong.
First published in Great Britain by ticktock Publishing Ltd., The Offices in the Square, Hadlow, Tonbridge, Kent TN11 0DD, Great Britain.
Picture Credits: Allsport: IFC, 2–3c, 3tr, 4tl, 7tr, 8tl, 10–11c, 12cl, 14tl, 14–15c, 16–17b, 18–19c, 19tr, 20–21, 22–23c, 23tr, 24bl, 24–25t, 26–27c, 27br, 28bl, 28–29c, 30–31b, 31tl; SIPA press: 16–17t; Vandystadt: 6–7c, 8–9c, 13–13c.
Picture research by Image Select.
Library of Congress Cataloging-in-Publication Data
Page, Jason.
Combat : fencing, judo, wrestling, boxing, taekwondo, and lots, lots more / by Jason Page.
p. cm. — (Zeke's Olympic pocket guide)
Summary: Describes the combat events of the Olympic Games and previews the athletic competition at the 2000 Summer Olympics in Sydney, Australia.
Includes index.
ISBN 0-8225-5055-5 (pbk. : alk. paper)
1. Fencing--Juvenile literature. 2. Wrestling--Juvenile literature. 3. Boxing--Juvenile literature. 4. Martial arts--Juvenile literature. 5. Olympics--Juvenile literature. [1. Fencing. 2. Wrestling. 3. Boxing. 4. Martial arts. 5. Olympics.] I. Title. II. Series.
GV 1147 .P34 2000
796.8--dc21
00-008099